INSIDE!

YOUR AWESOME MATCH ANNUAL 2012!

MATCH! ANNUAL 2012

BEST VALUE! THE ONLY FOOTY ANNUAL WORTH BUYING!

INSIDE >> Prem v Europe Face-off! >> Posters! >> Moments of the Year! >> Cartoons! >> Quizzes! >> Funny pics & loads more!

PREM v EUROPE 22

STARS AND THEIR CARS

D0938135

THE RONALDO STORY

MATCH CHECKS OUT THE BIGGEST STORIES FROM THE REAL MADRID & PORTUGAL WINGER'S AWESOME CAREER!

CRISTIANO RONALDO DOS SANTOS AVEIRO WAS BORN IN FUNCHAL, MADEIRA ON FEBRUARY 5, 1985. AFTER PLAYING FOR AMATEUR SIDE ANDORINHA, RONALDO JOINED LOCAL SIDE NACIONAL WHEN HE WAS TEN.

RONALDO THEN JOINED SPORTING LISBON'S YOUTH ACADEMY IN 1997 AND SET A CLUB RECORD OF PLAYING FOR THE UNDER-16, UNDER-17, UNDER-18 AND B-TEAM

I'M THE BEST NO.7 EVER!

CRISTIANO RONALDO 42

EURO 2012 50

BEST MOMENTS OF 2011 60

TOP TEN 68

CARTOONS 72

MATCH! MATES WITH THE STARS! OUT EVERY TUESDAY!

MESSI!

THE BEST PLAYER ON THE PLANET!

BARÇA's superstar had a year to remember in 2011!

Barcelona's awesome line-up is packed with stars like David Villa, Gerard Pique, Xavi, Andres Iniesta and Pedro, but Lionel Messi was untouchable in 2011! Join MATCH as we look back at the Nou Camp legend's best moments of the year!

FCB

World Player Of The Year!

Messi began 2011 in spectacular style as he won the FIFA Ballon d'Or in January! Leo beat Barcelona team-mates Xavi and Andres Iniesta to bag the most famous player award in footy!

La Liga record!

Barcelona broke a La Liga record as they bagged their 16th victory in a row in February! Messi scored a hat-trick as Pep Guardiola's side thrashed Atletico Madrid 3-0!

Agony for Arsenal!

Barcelona had it all to do against Arsenal in the Champions League last 16 back in March, but Messi scored twice at the Nou Camp as Barça won 4-3 on aggregate!

Destroying Real!

In the Champo League semi-finals against Real Madrid, Messi scored two incredible first-leg goals at the Bernabeu to put Barcelona in charge against their big rivals!

Kings of Europe!

Messi saved his first goal for Barcelona on English soil for the Champions League final! Leo smashed the ball past Edwin van der Sar in Barça's 3-1 win against Man. United!

Stat Attack!
Lionel Messi 2010-11

Games	53
Goals	50

MATCH!
Behind the scenes in the weird world of footy!

CAN SOMEONE GET ME A PIE?

GERRARD'S AWAY DAY!

LIVERPOOL: Injured captain Steven Gerrard joined the Liverpool fans in the stands at Villa Park for their final game of last season. He was way too busy posing for photos and chatting to watch the game properly, though!

OF COURSE WE MISS TORRES!

Maccy VDV'S

NO-ONE MESSES WITH MY BABY!

MARIO'S FISHY WHEELS!

I EAT HERE SO MUCH THEY GAVE ME A FREE CLOWN SUIT!

VAN DER VAART

TOTTENHAM: When MATCH hung out with Rafael van der Vaart last season he told us he loves fast food! The Holland star said, "I like to eat at McDonald's! My son also likes it, so I pretend to get it for him!" Don't tell Harry Redknapp!

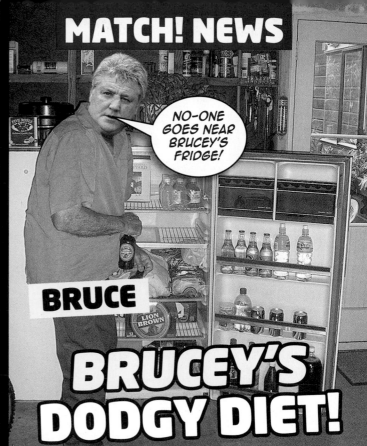

NO-ONE GOES NEAR BRUCEY'S FRIDGE!

BRUCE

BRUCEY'S DODGY DIET!

SUNDERLAND: Steve Bruce wants to drop a few pounds in 2012, but knows it's going to be tough. Brucey said, "I'm going to lose some weight if I can, but I do like a pork pie with a can of beer, and pork sandwiches with a bit of mustard. Marvellous!"

LADY THEO!

THESE HEELS ARE KILLING ME!

ARSENAL: Theo Walcott said he felt like Lady Gaga after bagging loads of attention from screaming fans during The Gunners' tour of Asia last summer. Hopefully he doesn't start dressing up like her, too!

MAN. CITY: When Mario Balotelli got back from City's US tour last summer, he found a rotten fish in the back of his flashy Maserati! None of his team-mates owned up to the smelly prank!

MX60 AKJ

WHO DID IT?

6'0"	6'0"
5'5"	5'5"
5'0"	5'0"
4'5"	4'5"
4'0"	4'0"
3'5"	3'5"
3'0"	3'0"
DE JONG MIDFIELDER	**HART** GOALKEEPER
6'0"	6'0"
5'5"	5'5"
5'0"	5'0"
4'5"	4'5"
4'0"	4'0"
3'5"	3'5"
3'0"	3'0"
SWP WINGER	**MILNER** MIDFIELDER

Thiago Alcantara?

MATCH tells you all you need to know about Spain's next midfield superstar!

WHAT'S HIS FULL NAME?

Thiago Alcantara do Nascimento

HE HAS A BUY-OUT CLAUSE OF...

£81m

HOW TALL IS HE?

5ft 8ins

HOW OLD IS HE?

20

WHO DOES HE PLAY LIKE?

Xavi

WHAT'S HE GOOD AT?

Passing
Shooting
Vision
Creativity

WHO'S MOST LIKELY TO SIGN HIM?

Arsenal

WHAT BOOTS DOES HE WEAR?

Nike CTR360 Maestri II

WHO'S HIS DAD?

1994 World Cup winner, Mazinho

WHAT POSITION DOES HE PLAY?

Central midfield

WHO DOES HE PLAY FOR?

Spain & Barcelona

WHAT'S HE WON?

La Liga 2009, 2010 & 2011
Spanish Supercup 2010
Champions League 2011
Under-17 Euro Championship 2008
Under-21 Euro Championship 2011

LEGENDS

2011

WILSHERE

THE BIG QUIZ!

sport switch!

Name the legendary Prem striker who has retired from footy to take up playing basketball!

5 POINTS FOR CORRECT ANSWER

MY SCORE
5

5 QUESTIONS ON...

DAVID LUIZ!

1 Which huge Portuguese club did Chelsea sign Luiz from in January?

2 Which international team does the classy centre-back play for - Argentina, Brazil or Paraguay?

3 How much did Chelsea pay for the mega-haired defender - £11 million or £21 million?

4 How many goals did Luiz score for Chelsea in the 2010-11 season?

5 Against which Premier League club did Luiz score his first goal for The Blues back in March?

4 POINTS FOR EACH CORRECT ANSWER

MY SCORE
20

BOGUS BADGES!

Which clubs do these badges belong to?

2 POINTS FOR EACH CORRECT ANSWER

MY SCORE
10

1. ....
2. ....

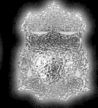

3. ....
4. ....
5. ....

WHO AM I?

Can you work out the mystery Prem star from these three clues?

THE MYSTERY PREM STAR IS...

1 I'm a 28-year-old midfielder who's also played in La Liga!

2 I joined my current club for £24 million in July 2010!

3 I play in the same Prem and international side as my brother!

5 POINTS FOR CORRECT ANSWER

MY SCORE
5

NAME THE TEAM!

Remember England's team from their Euro 2012 qualifier against Switzerland in June?

UEFA EURO 2012™ QUALIFIER
ENGLAND v SWITZERLAND
VAUXHALL
4 June 2011 Wembley Stadium

4 POINTS FOR EACH CORRECT ANSWER
MY SCORE
40

1. Arsenal ★ Winger

2. Man. City ★ Winger

3. Chelsea ★ Centre-back

4. Man. United ★ Centre-back
RIO FERDINAND

5. Aston Villa ★ Striker

6. Chelsea ★ Midfielder

7. Tottenham ★ Midfielder

8. Chelsea ★ Left-back

9. Man. City ★ Goalkeeper

10. Liverpool ★ Right-back

11. Arsenal ★ Midfielder

FLASHBACK!

5 POINTS FOR EACH CORRECT ANSWER
MY SCORE
20

Can you name all four of the Premier League stars in these dodgy old pics?

THE PREM STAR IS...

THE PREM STAR IS...

THE PREM STAR IS...

THE PREM STAR IS...

ANSWERS PAGE 94

WORDSEARCH!

Can you find all 25 world superstars hiding in the massive grid below?

```
Z R M I Z V A Z E B T B R X H F Z I W O
C I N P B X G O R O N A L D O F O J C E
E W S I J Y S H Q C H K M I A O R O R O
V I I Z D E V L C O B S N S A W F O N N
G F I L V R F M H T Z N X R Y C T F Q G
M U J L S P O N W H H E Z V K S S A T O
L N A G B H I G L A E I D F A V P B C M
S H Q T I T E A B Z D J W P I B C R X E
Y P U S U R B R H A U D V P B W O E X Z
X C S O N Z R V E R K E J A R H E G N Q
G E M W M I S A W D H R C E A T N A E B
M N T T K T S L X R U V A D H T T S Y A
M A O Q K R A D X B L T V Y I K R R M L
K M U B M D N E W F K T A R M C A O A E
J Y R Y F T C S L C Q H N D O X O O R T
O N E B O C H Q V W C G I E V A U N N O
M W M C I U E P O V I L L A I V O E S O
F L W Z E E Z W N V X Q D G C I O Y J D
```

Alves	Eto'o	Ibrahimovic	Pastore	Toure
Bale	Fabregas	Luiz	Ronaldo	Valdes
Cavani	Gomez	Messi	Rooney	Villa
Coentrao	Hazard	Moutinho	Sanchez	Wilshere
Drogba	Hulk	Neymar	Sneijder	Xavi

ANSWERS ON PAGE 94!

LEGENDS 2011

ROONEY

MANCHESTER UNITED

= CLASSIC MATCH 2011 =

 **Newcastle** — **4 : 4** — **Arsenal**

Barton 68, 83 (pens);
Best 75; Tiote 87

Walcott 1; Djourou 3;
Van Persie 10, 26

Date: February 5 **Stadium:** St. James' Park **Tournament:** Premier League

What happened? Arsenal looked like they'd wrapped up all three points by half-time as they shot into a 4-0 lead, but Newcastle had other ideas! Two penalties from Joey Barton, a Leon Best strike and an unbelievable volley from midfielder Cheik Tiote lifted the roof off St. James' Park in one of the best comebacks the Prem's ever seen!

QUESTION 1

True or False? England striker Andy Carroll played up front for Newcastle in this match!

....

QUESTION 2

Which Arsenal player was sent off early in the second half?

....

QUESTION 3

After how many seconds did Arsenal's lightning forward Theo Walcott open the scoring – 24, 34 or 44?

....

QUESTION 4

Which international team does Cheik Tiote play for – Algeria, South Africa or Ivory Coast?

....

QUESTION 5

Who was the manager of Newcastle in this match – Chris Hughton or Alan Pardew?

....

QUESTION 6

Argentina's Fabricio Coloccini played at centre-back in this match, but what shirt number does he wear for The Magpies?

....

ANSWERS! 1. False – he'd already signed for Liverpool; 2. Abou Diaby; 3. 44 seconds; 4. Ivory Coast; 5. Alan Pardew; 6. No.2.

STARS & THEIR CARS!

MATCH reveals the flashiest motors in the world, and the footy stars who drive them!

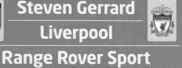

Steven Gerrard 	► **Costs:** £62,000
Liverpool	► **0-60:** 5.9 seconds
Range Rover Sport	► **Top Speed:** 140mph

David Beckham
LA Galaxy
Ferrari 612 Scaglietti
- ► **Costs:** £222,000
- ► **0-60:** 4.3 seconds
- ► **Top Speed:** 199mph

Anderson
Man. United
Mercedes SLS
- ► **Costs:** £158,000
- ► **0-60:** 3.8 seconds
- ► **Top Speed:** 197mph

Mario Balotelli
Man. City
Maserati GTS
- ► **Costs:** £78,500
- ► **0-60:** 5.2 seconds
- ► **Top Speed:** 177mph

Dirk Kuyt
Liverpool
Audi Q7
- ► **Costs:** £55,000
- ► **0-60:** 5.5 seconds
- ► **Top Speed:** 155mph

Nani
Man. United
Lamborghini Gallardo
- ► **Costs:** £115,000
- ► **0-60:** 4.3 seconds
- ► **Top Speed:** 192mph

Jermaine Pennant
Stoke
Aston Martin DBS
- ► **Costs:** £160,000
- ► **0-60:** 4.3 seconds
- ► **Top Speed:** 191mph

EXTRA-TIME!

Tackle these questions to find out how much you know about footy!

1 QPR defender Danny Gabbidon plays for which international team?

2 True or False? Chelsea left-back Ashley Cole has played for three London clubs during his career!

3 Which two massive teams went head-to-head in this season's Community Shield at Wembley?

4 How old is Liverpool keeper Pepe Reina – 29, 30 or 31 years old?

5 Which top car manufacturer sponsors the England team?

6 How much did Real Madrid pay for Brazil hero Kaka in 2009?

7 What's the name of the Adidas ball that will be used at the London 2012 Olympic Games?

8 Can you name the Chelsea legend who manages Championship side Brighton?

9 New Arsenal star Gervinho plays for which international team – Ivory Coast, Ghana or Cameroon?

10 Name the last English team to win the Champions League!

11 What position did Spurs finish in the Premier League in 2010-11?

12 Who was the Fulham manager before Martin Jol took over – Mark Hughes or Roy Hodgson?

13 Which giant sports company makes England's kit?

14 How many Premier League teams has deadly Aston Villa striker Darren Bent played for?

15 True or False? Norwich boss Paul Lambert won the Champions League back in 1997!

16 Name the Argentina boss who got sacked last summer!

17 Which Prem winger assisted the most goals in 2010-11?

18 Which League 1 club is nicknamed The Magpies?

19 Which two England players scored against Wales in March?

20 How many English titles have Man. United won?

21 Porto beat which team in the 2011 Europa League final?

22 What shirt number does Phil Jagielka wear for Everton?

23 Which Prem striker scored the winner in the Euro 2008 final?

24 Barry Ferguson joined which Championship club in July?

25 Fulham skipper Danny Murphy began his career at which club?

4 POINTS FOR EACH CORRECT ANSWER

MY SCORE
100

ANSWERS ON PAGE 94!

LEGENDS

2011

SUAREZ

PREM v EUROPE FACE-OFF!

MATCH is on a mission to find out which European league has the greatest players and gaffers on the planet!

PREM v EUROPE
MANAGERS

PEP GUARDIOLA

Club: Barcelona ★ **Age:** 40

Country: Spain

The former Barça captain hasn't stopped winning trophies since taking over from Frank Rijkaard in 2008! Guardiola has masterminded three La Liga titles and victories in two Champions League finals!

ARSENE WENGER

Club: Arsenal ★ **Age:** 61

Country: France

Wenger has won nothing with The Gunners since 2005, but he's still a Prem legend! He's won seven major trophies in 15 years, and his Invincibles won the title in 2004 without losing a single match!

JOSE MOURINHO

Club: Real Madrid ★ **Age:** 48

Country: Portugal

Mourinho wants more silverware after winning the Copa del Rey in his first season at the Bernabeu! His world-class footy brain has won the league in three countries and guided Inter to the treble in 2010!

ANDRE VILLAS-BOAS

Club: Chelsea ★ **Age:** 33

Country: Portugal

The Blues gaffer is one of the most talented young bosses in Europe! Villas-Boas loves his teams to attack and has been nicknamed the 'New Mourinho' after winning the treble with Porto last season!

SIR ALEX FERGUSON

Club: Man. United ★ **Age:** 69

Country: Scotland

Is there anything the legendary United gaffer hasn't won? Fergie is now the longest-serving manager ever at Old Trafford and has won an incredible 48 trophies at three different clubs during his career!

BEST OF THE REST!

ROBERTO MANCINI
Man. City

JURGEN KLOPP
Borussia Dortmund

MASSIMILIANO ALLEGRI
AC Milan

HARRY REDKNAPP
Tottenham

MANAGER
MY PICK...

....

MATCH! 23

SHAY GIVEN

Club: Aston Villa ★ **Age:** 35

Country: Republic Of Ireland

Given is one of the greatest Premier League keepers ever! The Ireland shot-stopper has made over 400 appearances in the top flight and will be looking to get back to his best after joining Aston Villa!

JOE HART

Club: Man. City ★ **Age:** 24

Country: England

England's No.1 has made sure he's Roberto Mancini's first-choice keeper after some electric displays! Hart's reflexes ensured Man. City's defence leaked the least goals in the Premier League last season!

PEPE REINA

Club: Liverpool ★ **Age:** 29

Country: Spain

Reina started every Premier League match in 2010-11! The Reds legend is strong, reliable and makes tons of incredible saves in every match! He even played his 150th game in a row for Liverpool back in May!

DAVID DE GEA

Club: Man. United ★ **Age:** 20

Country: Spain

United's new keeper has big boots to fill with legend Edwin van der Sar retiring last summer! After winning the European U-21 Championship, De Gea became the most expensive Premier League keeper of all time!

PETR CECH

Club: Chelsea ★ **Age:** 29

Country: Czech Republic

Chelsea's 2010-11 Player Of The Year kept 20 clean sheets as The Blues finished second in the Prem and reached the Champions League quarter-finals! He also made his 300th Prem appearance in March!

BEST OF THE REST!

CHRISTIAN ABBIATI
AC Milan

RON-ROBERT ZIELER
Hannover

MARK SCHWARZER
Fulham

HUGO LLORIS
Lyon

DIEGO LOPEZ
Villarreal

IKER CASILLAS

Club: Real Madrid ★ **Age:** 30

Country: Spain

Captain of Real Madrid and Spain, Casillas is one of Europe's greatest shot-stoppers ever! He's won four La Liga titles, two Champions League trophies, one Copa del Rey, Euro 2008 and the 2010 World Cup!

GIANLUIGI BUFFON

Club: Juventus ★ **Age:** 33

Country: Italy

Unbelievably Buffon's world-record £32.6 million move to Juventus in 2001 is still the highest fee ever paid for a keeper! He had an injury-hit 2010-11, but his reactions are still lightning and he bosses his area!

VICTOR VALDES

Club: Barcelona ★ **Age:** 29

Country: Spain

Barcelona are packed with attacking stars, but they couldn't have won La Liga and the Champo League in 2011 without Valdes' super saves! He's won La Liga's best goalkeeper award for the past three seasons!

MANUEL NEUER

Club: Bayern Munich ★ **Age:** 25

Country: Germany

After becoming Germany's No.1 at the 2010 World Cup, Neuer's career has gone from strength to strength! His saves helped Schalke reach the Champions League semi-finals and grabbed the attention of Bayern!

STEVE MANDANDA

Club: Marseille ★ **Age:** 26

Country: France

Marseille missed out on the title to Lille in 2011, but that didn't stop Mandanda being crowned Ligue 1's Keeper Of The Year! MATCH reckons he's ready to replace Hugo Lloris as France's first-choice keeper!

MAARTEN STEKELENBURG
Roma

ROMAN WEIDENFELLER
Borussia Dortmund

JULIO CESAR
Inter Milan

TIM HOWARD
Everton

GOALKEEPER
MY PICK...

....

PREM v EUROPE
CENTRE-BACKS

JOHN TERRY
Club: Chelsea ★ **Age:** 30
Country: England

JT made his 500th appearance for Chelsea last season! His leadership, bravery and strength scare the life out of strikers – no wonder England boss Fabio Capello gave him the captain's armband back in March!

VINCENT KOMPANY
Club: Man. City ★ **Age:** 25
Country: Belgium

Prem strikers must hate it when Kompany is on City's teamsheet! The Belgium centre-back reads the game like a legend, owns strikers with his power and pace, and has world-class positional play!

NEMANJA VIDIC
Club: Man. United ★ **Age:** 29
Country: Serbia

The Serbia powerhouse marked his first season as Man. United captain by leading his Red Devils team-mates to a record-breaking 19th title! Vidic was also shortlisted for the PFA Player Of The Year award!

DAVID LUIZ
Club: Chelsea ★ **Age:** 24
Country: Brazil

Chelsea's centre-back might have mad hair, but there's nothing crazy about his footy skills! Luiz loves crunching tackles, bringing the ball out of defence and powerful headers – he's JT's perfect partner!

RIO FERDINAND
Club: Man. United ★ **Age:** 32
Country: England

Is there any better centre-back partnership in the Prem than Rio and Vidic? The England star blasted back from the knee injury he picked up before last year's World Cup to win his fifth league title in 2011!

BEST OF THE REST!

PEPE
Real Madrid

ROLANDO
Porto

NEVEN SUBOTIC
Borussia Dortmund

RICARDO CARVALHO
Real Madrid

JAMIE CARRAGHER
Liverpool

MATS HUMMELS

Club: B. Dortmund ★ **Age:** 22

Country: Germany

Borussia Dortmund have Hummels to thank for helping crush the rest of the Bundesliga on the way to their seventh title! The ex-Bayern Munich star was like a brick wall at the back for Jurgen Klopp's side!

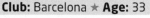

CARLES PUYOL

Club: Barcelona ★ **Age:** 33

Country: Spain

Puyol's power and leadership make him one of the hardest defenders in the world, even if he does have horror hair! The Spain legend has spent his whole career at the Nou Camp and has won everything!

GERARD PIQUE

Club: Barcelona ★ **Age:** 24

Country: Spain

Pique continued where he left off after winning the World Cup as Barcelona conquered La Liga and Europe! The Spain hero bossed the back four and even topped off his season by dating singer, Shakira!

THIAGO SILVA

Club: AC Milan ★ **Age:** 27

Country: Brazil

The Samba star rocked for AC Milan in 2010-11 as they won Serie A! Strikers across Europe couldn't deal with Silva's energy, last-ditch blocks and perfectly-timed tackles! We'd love to see him playing in the Prem!

DIEGO LUGANO

Club: PSG ★ **Age:** 30

Country: Uruguay

Lugano is a rock at the heart of the PSG and Uruguay defence! He's a true fighter, is unbeatable in the air and good on the deck! No wonder Uruguay were unstoppable at the Copa America last summer!

GIORGIO CHIELLINI
Juventus

ALESSANDRO NESTA
AC Milan

BREDE HANGELAND
Fulham

THOMAS VERMAELEN
Arsenal

CENTRE-BACKS
MY PICKS....

....
....
....

PREM v EUROPE
FULL-BACKS

BACARY SAGNA

Club: Arsenal ★ **Age:** 28

Country: France

Arsenal's awesome right-back had a quality 2010-11 for The Gunners and was picked in the PFA Team Of The Season! The speedy defender loves to break out from the back and has a great eye for a pass!

LEIGHTON BAINES

Club: Everton ★ **Age:** 26

Country: England

The Toffees' top left-back won't forget 2011 in a hurry! Baines' pinpoint crossing from the left caused Prem defenders nightmares as his 11 assists pushed David Moyes' side up to seventh in the table!

BRANISLAV IVANOVIC

Club: Chelsea ★ **Age:** 27

Country: Serbia

Ivanovic's third season at Stamford Bridge saw him play at right-back and in the middle alongside John Terry! He's powerful, tough to beat in one-on-ones and even loves popping up to grab vital goals!

ASHLEY COLE

Club: Chelsea ★ **Age:** 30

Country: England

The legendary Chelsea star is one of the greatest attacking full-backs on the planet! The England left-back destroys opponents with his rapid speed down the touchline, well-timed tackles and accurate crosses!

PATRICE EVRA

Club: Man. United ★ **Age:** 30

Country: France

After a disastrous World Cup in South Africa, Evra put it all behind him last season as United stormed to another Prem title! Evra loves getting forward and delivering dangerous balls into the box!

BEST OF THE REST!

MAICON
Inter Milan

ERIC ABIDAL
Barcelona

SERGIO RAMOS
Real Madrid

MAXWELL
Barcelona

TAYE TAIWO
AC Milan

PHILIPP LAHM

Club: Bayern Munich ★ **Age:** 27

Country: Germany

Bayern Munich really struggled last season, but captain Lahm is still one of the greatest full-backs in Europe! He's brilliant at using his pace and ball control to destroy defenders, before whipping in deadly crosses!

GREGORY VAN DER WIEL

Club: Ajax ★ **Age:** 23

Country: Holland

The Ajax full-back had a brilliant season as the Eredivisie title returned to Amsterdam! Van der Wiel loves breaking up attacks, and uses his incredible engine and speed to get forward down the wing!

DANI ALVES

Club: Barcelona ★ **Age:** 28

Country: Brazil

When the speedy right-back bursts forward, you know there's going to be goals! Alves leaves full-backs for dead, loves joining the attack and is a free-kick expert - check out his screamer for Brazil against Iran!

MARCELO

Club: Real Madrid ★ **Age:** 23

Country: Brazil

Real have become lethal down the left wing thanks to Marcelo and Cristiano Ronaldo's partnership! Marcelo made the left-back spot his own last season as Real beat rivals Barcelona in the Copa del Rey final!

FABIO COENTRAO

Club: Real Madrid ★ **Age:** 23

Country: Portugal

Loads of Europe's top clubs were chasing Coentrao's signature, but it was Real Madrid who beat them all to the Portugal international! The £26 million man has a brilliant left foot and frightening pace!

MARCEL SCHMELZER
Borussia Dortmund

GAEL CLICHY
Man. City

ALY CISSOKHO
Lyon

GLEN JOHNSON
Liverpool

FULL-BACKS
MY PICKS...

....

....

....

= CLASSIC MATCH 2011 =

Inter Milan
Stankovic 1; Milito 33

2 : 5

Schalke
Matip 17; Edu 40, 75;
Raul 53; Ranocchia 58 (og)

Date: April 5 **Stadium:** San Siro **Tournament:** Champions League QF first leg

What happened? No-one expected holders Inter Milan to ship five goals at home against Schalke - especially after Dejan Stankovic opened the scoring with a stunning volley from the halfway line! With the match level at 2-2 at the break, Schalke then scored three goals to go through to the semi-finals for the first time in their history!

QUESTION 1
What was the score between Inter Milan and Schalke in their quarter-final second leg match?
....

QUESTION 2
Raul joined Schalke from which European giants in July 2010?
....

QUESTION 3
True or False? Man. United beat Schalke in last season's Champions League semi-finals!
....

QUESTION 4

Can you name the awesome German international shot-stopper who played in goal for Schalke in this match?

....

QUESTION 5

Which Inter Milan defender was sent off in the second half of this match?

....

QUESTION 6

Name the legendary Inter Milan star who captained the Champions League holders in this awesome game!

....

THE BIG QUIZ!

flipped!

Which top Prem star has had his face messed up in this weird pic?

10 POINTS FOR CORRECT ANSWER

MY SCORE
10

5 QUESTIONS ON...

DARREN BENT!

1 At which Championship club did Bent begin his career – Brighton, Ipswich or Barnsley?

2 Which current League 1 club did the England striker play for between 2005 and 2007?

3 Against which South American team did Bent make his senior England debut back in 2006?

4 Bent scored his first Three Lions goal against which country in a Euro 2012 qualifier?

5 How much did Aston Villa pay Sunderland to sign the deadly England striker back in January?

2 POINTS FOR EACH CORRECT ANSWER

MY SCORE
10

MAN. UNITED QUIZ!

1 True or False? Old Trafford's nickname is the Theatre Of Dreams!

2 How many times have Man. United won the English league title - 17, 18 or 19?

3 Which top kit manufacturer make The Red Devils' awesome kit – Adidas, Umbro or Nike?

4 Name the Man. United and England legend who wears the No.5 shirt at Old Trafford!

5 How much did Man. United splash out on highly-rated star Phil Jones last summer?

2 POINTS FOR EACH CORRECT ANSWER

MY SCORE
10

STAR JUMBLE!

Which players' names are scrambled up?

2 POINTS FOR EACH CORRECT ANSWER

MY SCORE
10

Hen Vile Pill

Wipe Orient Gemed

Lined Jersey Sew

Jaws Rich Leek

Zebra Man Mike

WORDFIT!

Can you fit all 20 of these European teams into this giant grid?

REAL MADRID

2 POINTS FOR EACH CORRECT ANSWER

MY SCORE 40

Ajax	Celtic	Lille	Napoli	Schalke
Anderlecht	Chelsea	Liverpool	Olympiakos	Tottenham
Barcelona	FC Twente	Man. United	PSV	Udinese
Bayern Munich	Inter Milan	Marseille	Rangers	Villarreal

EURO GIANTS!

Can you guess which country these massive European clubs play footy in?

4 POINTS FOR EACH CORRECT ANSWER

MY SCORE 20

Lorient	Stuttgart	Fiorentina	Ajax	Real Mallorca

ANSWERS PAGE 94

THE RONALDO STORY

MATCH CHECKS OUT THE BIGGEST STORIES FROM THE REAL MADRID & PORTUGAL WINGER'S AWESOME CAREER!

CRISTIANO RONALDO DOS SANTOS AVEIRO WAS BORN IN FUNCHAL, MADEIRA ON FEBRUARY 5, 1985. AFTER PLAYING FOR AMATEUR SIDE ANDORINHA, RONALDO JOINED LOCAL SIDE NACIONAL WHEN HE WAS TEN.

RONALDO THEN JOINED SPORTING LISBON'S YOUTH ACADEMY IN 1997 AND SET A CLUB RECORD OF PLAYING FOR THE UNDER-16, UNDER-17, UNDER-18 AND B-TEAM IN THE SAME SEASON!

WHO ARE YOU, OLD MAN?

I'M THE BEST NO.7 EVER!

HE CAME TO THE ATTENTION OF EUROPE'S TOP CLUBS PLAYING FOR PORTUGAL AT THE 2002 UNDER-17 EUROPEAN CHAMPIONSHIP. A YEAR LATER RONALDO WAS ON HIS WAY TO MAN. UNITED IN A £12.24 MILLION DEAL!

WEARING MAN. UNITED'S FAMOUS NO.7 SHIRT PREVIOUSLY WORN BY DAVID BECKHAM AND ERIC CANTONA, RONALDO CAME OFF THE BENCH TO MAKE HIS PREMIER LEAGUE DEBUT IN A MASSIVE 4-0 WIN AGAINST BOLTON IN AUGUST 2003.

THE BEST OF...
twitter

MATCH looks back at the craziest tweets of the year!

Wow... someone is letting off some lively farts on the team coach. Confined spaces and farts are not a good mix! My money's on Jonny Evans!

@rioferdy5
Rio Ferdinand – Man. United

Already won player of the month and best buy of the season, now also nominated for player of the year. I'm very proud!

@rafvdvaart
Rafael van der Vaart – Tottenham

Have assembled a game of head tennis in terminal! Holden + Coyle 2-0 Klasnic + @marcoalonso28! Easy easy! Champs!

@Stuholden
Stuart Holden – Bolton

Home at 2am. Kids jumping on me at 5.58am. Great start to the day.

@fizzer18
Phil Neville – Everton

Had a great laugh watching Hangover 2 last night! At one point I was drinking water and it fell out of my mouth when Stu was singing.

@cesc4official
Cesc Fabregas – Barcelona

I'm very proud of this weekend. I wasn't sure I'd score twice, and match Hugo Sanchez and Zarra's record.

@Cristiano
Cristiano Ronaldo – Real Madrid

@rioferdy5 can't believe me and jonny are getting the blame for farting. When @themichaelowen is sitting there wafting and grinning.

@WayneRooney
Wayne Rooney – Man. United

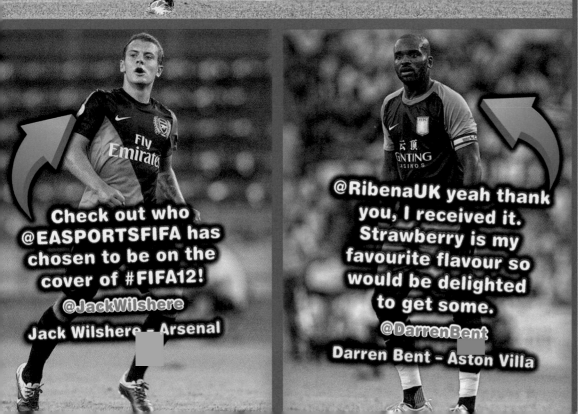

Check out who @EASPORTSFIFA has chosen to be on the cover of #FIFA12!

@JackWilshere
Jack Wilshere – Arsenal

@RibenaUK yeah thank you, I received it. Strawberry is my favourite flavour so would be delighted to get some.

@DarrenBent
Darren Bent – Aston Villa

Twitter Trouble!

Check out this year's most memorable rants!

Name: Joey Barton
Club: QPR
When: After losing with former club Newcastle before the start of last season.

"If only we as players could tell the fans exactly how it is, without them above fining us lots of money. There will be a time and a place."

Result: Given a free transfer!

Name: Aaron Lennon
Club: Tottenham
When: After missing April's 4-0 defeat to Real Madrid in the Champions League.

"This is one day I did not want to miss. I will not be made a scapegoat saying they only knew just before kick-off. I fell ill on Sunday."

Result: Escaped punishment!

Name: Ryan Babel
Club: Hoffenheim
When: After ref Howard Webb sent off Liverpool's Steven Gerrard in the FA Cup third round, Babel photoshopped Webb's head onto a Man. United shirt.

"And they call him one of the best referees. That's a joke."

Result: Fined £10,000!

Name: Jack Wilshere
Club: Arsenal
When: After Abou Diaby was sent off against Newcastle back in February.

"Inconsistent refereeing needs to stop. It's killing the game. If Diaby goes, what's the difference between that and Nolan on our keeper?"

Result: Escaped punishment!

EXTRA-TIME!

Tackle these questions to find out how much you know about footy!

1 True or False? West Brom play their home games at The Baggies!

2 Which Premier League team is the furthest north - Newcastle, Sunderland, Wolves or Bolton?

3 Man. United goal machine Javier Hernandez plays for which international team - Mexico or USA?

4 Atalanta, Siena and Genoa play footy in which country?

5 What first name links Vermaelen, Sorensen and Hitzlsperger?

6 Which Championship side does Sven-Goran Eriksson manage?

7 Soccer Saturday presenter Jeff Stelling supports which team - Exeter, Torquay or Hartlepool?

8 Which Chelsea player scored the most goals last season - Kalou, Drogba, Anelka or Malouda?

9 True or False? Speedy right-back Micah Richards has spent his entire footy career with Man. City!

10 England legend David Beckham plays for which MLS team?

11 Which keeper joined Aston Villa from Man. City last summer?

12 Who scored Man. United's goal in last season's Champions League final against Barcelona?

13 Name the Scotland striker who joined Cardiff from Bursaspor!

14 How old is Bolton striker Kevin Davies - 34, 35 or 36 years old?

15 By how many points did Man. United win the Premier League title last season?

16 True or False? Wolves boss Mick McCarthy used to be the Republic Of Ireland captain!

17 Which Prem team scored the least amount of goals in 2010-11?

18 Bolton play their home games at which awesome stadium?

19 Swansea's Brendan Rodgers has managed which two other clubs?

20 What is Norwich's nickname - The Canaries or The Yellows?

21 Who wears the No.3 shirt for London mega club Tottenham?

22 Which Spain star has won more caps - Xavi or Xabi Alonso?

23 Which Liverpool new boy wears the No.19 shirt for The Reds?

24 Robert Huth and Jon Walters play for which Prem club?

25 True or False? Jose Mourinho has won the Champions League trophy with three different clubs!

4 POINTS FOR EACH CORRECT ANSWER

MY SCORE
100

ANSWERS ON PAGE 94!

LEGENDS

2011

AGUERO

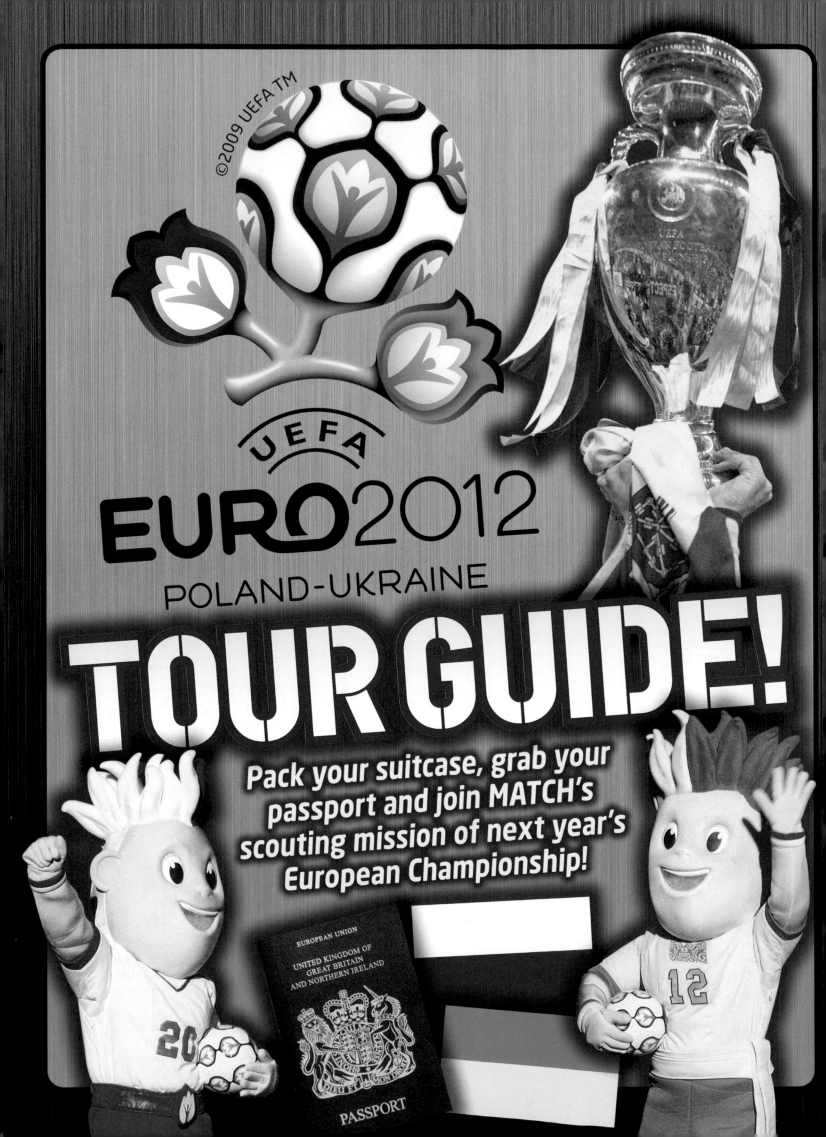

POLAND

PGE Arena
Capacity: 40,000
Fab Fact: The most northern stadium at Euro 2012 looks awesome! The outside is meant to look like amber, which is found locally!

City Stadium
POZNAN
Capacity: 40,000
Fab Fact: This enormous stadium is home to Lech Poznan! The Railwaymen played Man. City in last season's Europa League!

National Stadium
WARSAW
Capacity: 50,000
Fab Fact: This cool stadium hosts the opening match of the tournament and will be the future home of the Poland national team!

Municipal Stadium
WROCLAW
Capacity: 40,000
Fab Fact: The fourth Polish stadium is meant to look like a Chinese lantern, plus it'll be part of a complex that includes a casino!

MATCH REPORT!

POLAND'S CHAMPIONS: Wisla Krakow

BIGGEST TEAMS:
Legia Warsaw, Wisla Krakow and Lech Poznan

FAMOUS PLACES:
Warsaw, Krakow and Katowice

FAMOUS CELEBS: Wojciech Szczesny, Jerzy Dudek, Marie Curie and the Warner Brothers

WEIRDEST SPORT: Warsaw hosted the crazy Canoe Polo International Cup last summer!

WORST FOOD: Polish people love eating Flaki, a soup which is made from cows' stomachs!

UKRAINE

KIEV

Olympic Stadium
Capacity: 60,000
Fab Fact: Kiev's massive Olympic Stadium is the biggest at Euro 2012, will have a see-through roof and hosts the final on July 1!

LVIV

New Lviv Stadium
Capacity: 30,000
Fab Fact: The architects behind Lviv's cool stadium are the same ones who designed Klagenfurt's Hypo-Arena for Euro 2008!

MATCH REPORT!

UKRAINE'S CHAMPIONS: Shakhtar Donetsk

BIGGEST TEAMS:
Dynamo Kiev and Shakhtar Donetsk

FAMOUS PLACES:
Kiev, Kharkiv and Dnipropetrovsk

FAMOUS CELEBS: Andriy Shevchenko, the Klitschkos and Mila Kunis (Meg in Family Guy)

WEIRDEST SPORT: An international tractor racing event was held in Simferopol last year!

WORST FOOD: Pierogi. A dough stuffed with potatoes, sauerkraut, ground meat and cheese!

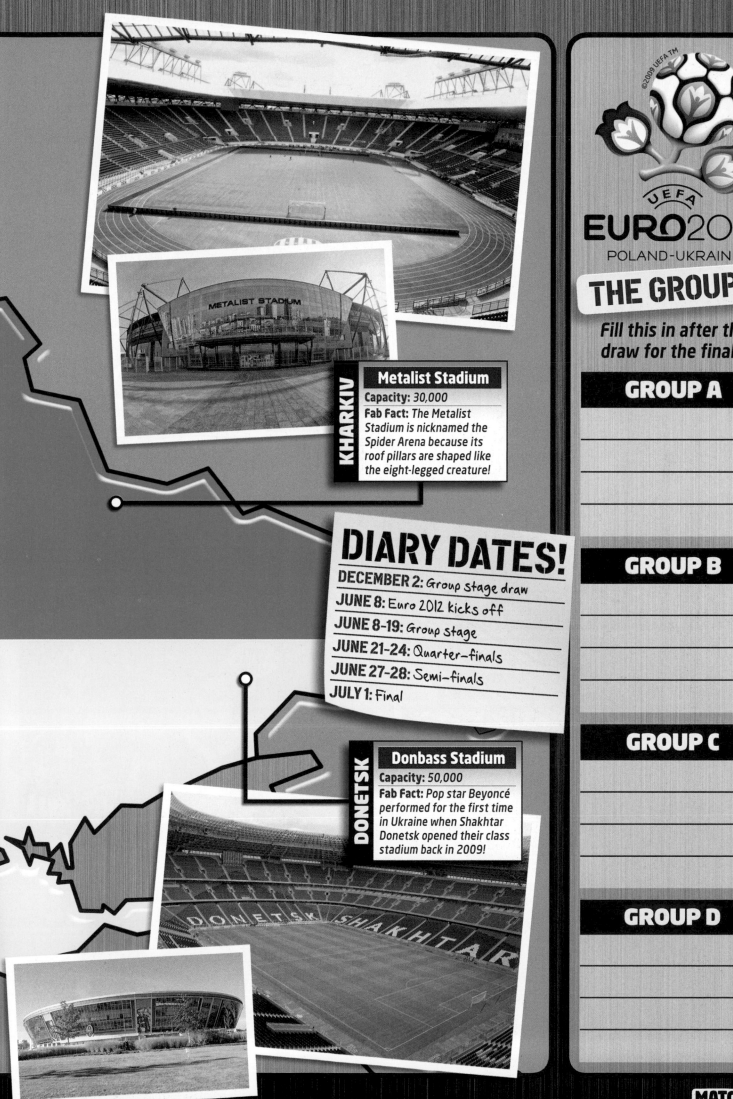

KHARKIV

Metalist Stadium

Capacity: 30,000

Fab Fact: The Metalist Stadium is nicknamed the Spider Arena because its roof pillars are shaped like the eight-legged creature!

DIARY DATES!

DECEMBER 2: Group stage draw

JUNE 8: Euro 2012 kicks off

JUNE 8-19: Group stage

JUNE 21-24: Quarter-finals

JUNE 27-28: Semi-finals

JULY 1: Final

DONETSK

Donbass Stadium

Capacity: 50,000

Fab Fact: Pop star Beyoncé performed for the first time in Ukraine when Shakhtar Donetsk opened their class stadium back in 2009!

©2009 UEFA TM

UEFA

EURO 2012
POLAND-UKRAINE

THE GROUPS

Fill this in after the draw for the finals!

GROUP A

GROUP B

GROUP C

GROUP D

THE AWESOME ADVENTURES OF MATCHMAN

LEGENDS

2011

FACTFILE!

Age: 30
Club: Chelsea
Position: Left-back
Value: £20 million
Country: England
Footy Fact! The England defender was named Chelsea's Player Of The Season in 2010-11!

COLE

THE BIG QUIZ!

sport switch!

Name the class Prem defender who has retired from footy to become a middleweight boxer!

10 POINTS FOR CORRECT ANSWER

MY SCORE **10**

fellaini's BARBERSHOP!

THE HIDDEN STAR IS...

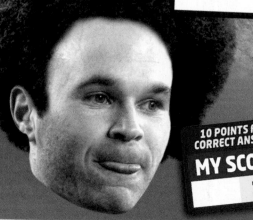

10 POINTS FOR CORRECT ANSWER

MY SCORE **10**

5 QUESTIONS ON...
THEO WALCOTT!

1 In what year did Theo join Arsenal from Southampton - 2005, 2006 or 2007?

2 Against which team did Walcott make his Premier League debut - Liverpool, Chelsea or Aston Villa?

3 Walcott scored his first Gunners goal in the 2007 League Cup final, but can you remember which London team it was against?

4 Walcott scored a hat-trick for England against which country in a World Cup qualifier in 2008?

5 What legendary shirt number does the rapid winger wear for Arsenal – No.8, No.14 or No.23?

4 POINTS FOR EACH CORRECT ANSWER

MY SCORE **20**

STADIUM GAME!

2 POINTS FOR EACH CORRECT ANSWER

MY SCORE **10**

Which clubs play here?

1. IBROX STADIUM

2. THE BERNABEU

3. ST. JAMES' PARK

4. LOFTUS ROAD

5. DW STADIUM

CROSSWORD!

Use the clues to fill in this massive crossword grid!

ACROSS

3. 2011 Copa America champs! (7)
4. Winners of the 2011 Under-21 European Championship! (5)
6. Top Championship club that plays at the AMEX Stadium! (8)
9. Prem team Nigel Reo-Coker and Zat Knight play for! (6)
12. Nickname of Southend! (3,9)
14. Championship club Charlie Adam joined Liverpool from! (9)
16. Prem club Gael Givet and Michel Salgado play for! (9)

DOWN

1. 2014 World Cup hosts! (6)
2. Arsenal and Holland striker, Robin ___ _____! (3,6)
5. Europa League holders! (5)
6. Surname of Man. City striker, Mario _____! (9)
7. Celtic's nickname! (3,5)
8. Barcelona's top stadium! (3,4)
9. Euro giants Alexis Sanchez signed for last summer! (9)
10. Manager of Prem new boys Norwich, Paul _____! (7)
11. Team that Clarence Seedorf and Alexandre Pato play for! (2,5)
13. Reigning Prem champs! (3,6)
15. Fulham's awesome stadium, _____ Cottage! (6)
17. Massive Championship club managed by Simon Grayson! (5)
18. Chelsea's Czech Republic international goalkeeper! (4)

2 POINTS FOR EACH CORRECT ANSWER

MY SCORE **40**

TRANSFER TRACKER!

Fill in the gaps in the career of James Milner!

5 POINTS FOR EACH CORRECT ANSWER

MY SCORE **10**

2002-04 Leeds

2003 Swindon (loan)

2004-08

2008-2010

2010-Now Man. City

ANSWERS PAGE 94

THE MAT

SHELVEY
VOLDEMORT

SUAREZ
DONKEY

BERBATOV
DRACULA

CH LAB!

BRUCE
WIGGUM

COLOCCINI
SHEEP

REDKNAPP
BULLDOG

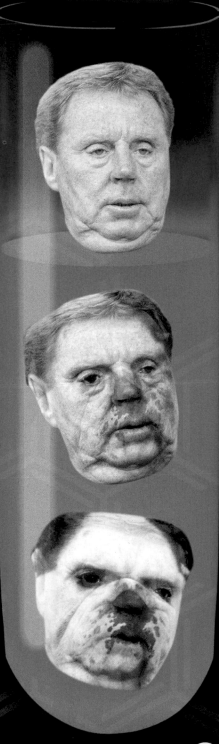

MOMENTS OF THE YEAR!

MATCH looks back at the 25 craziest footy stories from 2011! Check them all out...

Gattuso Goes Nuts!

After purs shocked the San Siro with a 1-0 win against AC Milan in the Champions League, Gennaro Gattuso went crazy and headbutted Spurs assistant Joe Jordan!

Stevenage Stun Newcastle!

LEAGUE 2 NEW BOYS STEVENAGE DUMPED PREMIER LEAGUE GIANTS NEWCASTLE OUT OF THE FA CUP AFTER THRASHING THE MAGPIES 3-1 IN THE THIRD ROUND!

Mega Moves!

The British transfer record was absolutely smashed in January! Andy Carroll joined Liverpool from Newcastle for £35 million and Chelsea splashed out a crazy £50 million on Fernando Torres!

King Kenny Returns!

Liverpool were 12th in the table when Anfield legend Kenny Dalglish took over from Roy Hodgson back in January! Ten victories from their remaining 18 matches saw The Reds just miss out on a Europa League spot!

Goal Of The Season!

Man. United fans went mental when Wayne Rooney scored a sensational overhead kick against rivals Man. City at Old Trafford in February! It's one of the best Prem goals ever!

Red-faced Ref!

BIRMINGHAM'S JORDON MUTCH DIDN'T KNOW WHERE TO LOOK WHEN REF PETER WALTON SHOWED HIM AN IMAGINARY YELLOW CARD AGAINST EVERTON IN MARCH!

Awesome Arsenal!

Two goals in five minutes from Robin van Persie and Andrey Arshavin helped The Gunners come from behind to beat Barcelona in the Champions League in February! It was one of the greatest matches of all time at The Emirates!

Crazy Cup Final!

Birmingham won their first trophy since 1963 as Obafemi Martins scored a last-gasp winner in the Carling Cup final after a mix up between Arsenal keeper Wojciech Szczesny and Laurent Koscielny!

Spurs Storm Back!

Arsenal's hopes of a first Prem title since 2004 were wrecked as they let a two-goal lead slip against Spurs! Tom Huddlestone scored a stunner, before Rafael van der Vaart equalised from the penalty spot in a 3-3 draw!

Old Firm Bust-up!

It all kicked off between Celtic and Rangers at Parkhead in the Scottish Cup! Neil Lennon and Ally McCoist had to be pulled apart, plus Rangers had Steven Whittaker, Madjid Bougherra and El Hadji Diouf all sent off!

RVP Sees Red!

ROBIN VAN PERSIE SAW RED AGAINST BARCA WHEN HE DIDN'T STOP FOR THE REF'S WHISTLE! HE SAID HE DIDN'T HEAR IT BECAUSE THE NOU CAMP WAS TOO NOISY!

Magical Messi!

The World Player Of The Year scored twice against Real Madrid in their Champions League semi-final first leg! After opening the scoring, he went on a 30-yard run, beat four Real players and buried the ball past Iker Casillas!

Stoke Batter Bolton!

The Potters reached the FA Cup final for the first time ever after thrashing Bolton 5-0 at Wembley! Stoke didn't look back after Matthew Etherington opened the scoring after 11 minutes!

Mourinho's Marching Orders!

THE REAL MADRID BOSS WAS SENT TO THE STANDS AFTER PEPE SAW RED AGAINST BARCELONA IN THE CHAMPIONS LEAGUE! REAL WENT ON TO LOSE THE MATCH 2-0!

Cup Slip-up!

Real Madrid celebrated in style after beating Barcelona to win the Copa del Rey! No-one should have given the cup to Sergio Ramos, though – he dropped it off the top of a double-decker bus!

Emirates Epic!

After Jamie Carragher picked up a serious head injury against Arsenal in April, Robin van Persie's 98th-minute penalty looked to have won the match! But Dirk Kuyt equalised from the spot 12 minutes into stoppage time! Crazy!

Milan Moonwalk!

KEVIN-PRINCE BOATENG BUSTED OUT MICHAEL JACKSON'S COOL MOONWALK DANCE AFTER AC MILAN WON THEIR FIRST SERIE A TITLE FOR SEVEN YEARS BACK IN MAY!

Toure Wins The Cup!

Man. City midfielder Yaya Toure broke Stoke fans' hearts in the 130th FA Cup final at Wembley! His goal ended The Citizens' 35-year wait for a major trophy!

Hat-trick Hero!

Scott Sinclair's treble at Wembley in the Championship Play-Off final gave Swansea a 4-2 win against Reading! The Swans became the first team from Wales to reach the Prem!

The New Mourinho!

Everyone thought Guus Hiddink would take over at Chelsea when Carlo Ancelotti got sacked in May! But Roman Abramovich named Andre Villas-Boas as The Blues' new boss after he won the league and Europa League with Porto!

Survival Sunday!

The final day of the Prem season was well exciting! Five teams were in the scrap to avoid the drop, but it was Birmingham and Blackpool who joined relegated West Ham in the Championship!

Rooney's New Rug!

MAN. UNITED SUPERSTAR WAYNE ROONEY THOUGHT HE WAS GOING BALD AT JUST 25 YEARS OLD, SO HE SPLASHED OUT A WHOPPING £30,000 ON A HAIR TRANSPLANT!

Final Fight!

Following Santos' 2-1 win against Penarol in the Copa Libertadores final, both teams had a huge ruck! Highly-rated Santos and Brazil striker Neymar got involved in the big fight after the final whistle!

Mario Mucks Up!

Man. City striker Mario Balotelli was clear on goal in a pre-season friendly against LA Galaxy, but instead of shooting he backheeled the ball wide! Roberto Mancini hauled him off minutes later!

Midlands Move!

Fans of huge Midlands rivals Birmingham and Aston Villa couldn't believe it when boss Alex McLeish took over at Villa Park in June! He quit the Carling Cup holders by email!

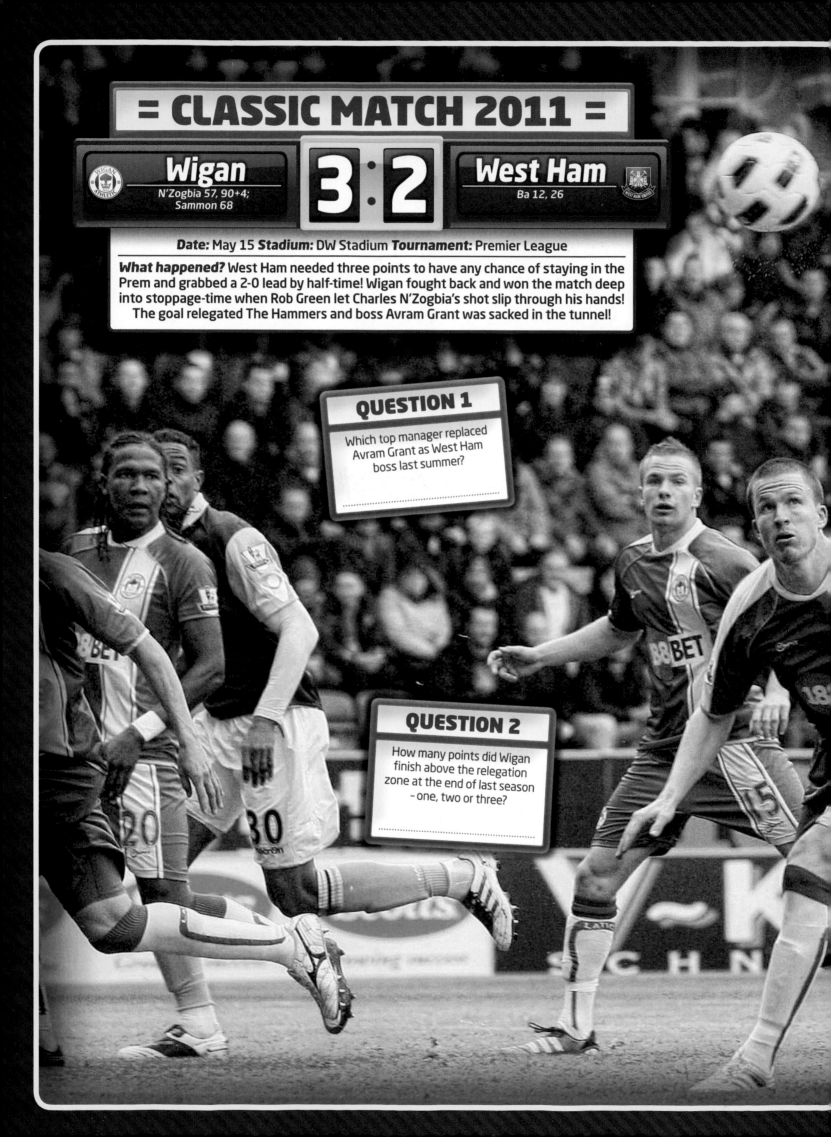

= CLASSIC MATCH 2011 =

Wigan 3 : 2 **West Ham**

N'Zogbia 57, 90+4;
Sammon 68

Ba 12, 26

Date: May 15 **Stadium:** DW Stadium **Tournament:** Premier League

What happened? West Ham needed three points to have any chance of staying in the Prem and grabbed a 2-0 lead by half-time! Wigan fought back and won the match deep into stoppage-time when Rob Green let Charles N'Zogbia's shot slip through his hands! The goal relegated The Hammers and boss Avram Grant was sacked in the tunnel!

QUESTION 1

Which top manager replaced Avram Grant as West Ham boss last summer?

....

QUESTION 2

How many points did Wigan finish above the relegation zone at the end of last season – one, two or three?

....

QUESTION 3

Which Premier League club snapped up former West Ham goal machine Demba Ba on a free transfer in June?

....

QUESTION 4

From which SPL club did Wigan sign striker Conor Sammon in January – Motherwell or Kilmarnock?

....

QUESTION 5

What was the name of Wigan's ground before it was renamed the DW Stadium in 2009?

....

QUESTION 6

True or False? Wigan boss Roberto Martinez used to play in midfield for The Latics!

ANSWERS! 1. Sam Allardyce; 2. Three; 3. Newcastle; 4. Kilmarnock; 5. JJB Stadium; 6. True.

TOP 10

CHAMPIONS LEAGUE MOMENTS OF 2011!

10

Shakhtar Donetsk beat Arsenal to the top of Group H to reach the knockout stage for the first time in their history! The Ukrainian side then beat Roma 6-2 in the last 16, before losing to Barça in the quarters!

9

For only the second time in the competition's history, a team overcame a first-leg home defeat to go through! Inter Milan lost 1-0 against Bayern Munich before winning 3-2 at the Allianz Arena!

8

Ryan Giggs rolled back the years against Chelsea at Stamford Bridge in the quarter-finals! He brought Michael Carrick's pass down like a legend, beat Jose Bosingwa and pulled the ball back for Wayne Rooney to hit the winner!

7

Midfield legend Paul Scholes played his last game for Man. United in the Champions League final! Scholesy came on for the last 14 minutes in his 676th appearance for Sir Alex Ferguson's side!

6

After topping Group A in their first ever Champions League campaign, Spurs then beat Italian giants AC Milan 1-0 in the last 16! Striker Peter Crouch scored the winner at the San Siro!

5

After totally outclassing Man. United 3-1 to win their fourth European Cup, Barcelona defender Gerard Pique cut down the Wembley nets to take pieces home with him as a souvenir of their awesome win!

4

Jose Mourinho was sent to the stands in a fiery first leg El Clasico against Barça in the semi-finals! The Real Madrid boss was furious after Pepe was shown a red card for a high tackle on Dani Alves!

3

Tottenham fans couldn't wait for their quarter-final first leg against Real Madrid, but it all went wrong at the Bernabeu! Striker Peter Crouch saw red for getting two yellow cards in the first 15 minutes and Spurs ended up getting battered 4-0!

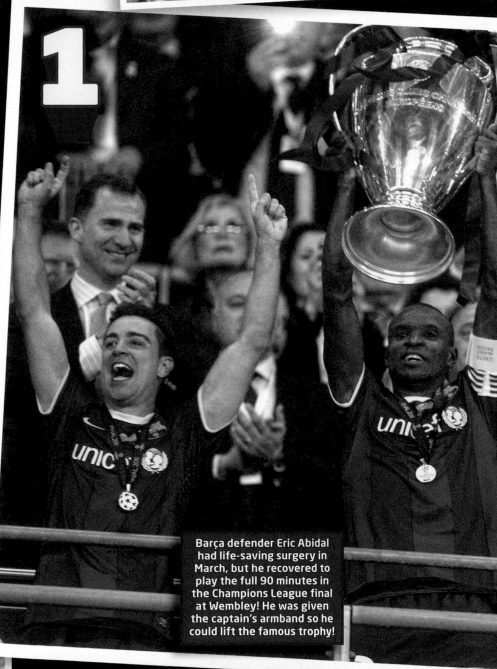

1

Barça defender Eric Abidal had life-saving surgery in March, but he recovered to play the full 90 minutes in the Champions League final at Wembley! He was given the captain's armband so he could lift the famous trophy!

2

Nobody gave Schalke a chance in the Champions League last season, but they ended up getting to the semi-finals! Euro goalscoring legend Raul set a new UEFA competitions record as he reached 73 goals!

SNAPPED! BEST OF 2011!

Barcelona's players lost it when Cesc Fabregas finally signed last summer!

THERE'S NOTHING WRONG WITH THEM!

MATCH can't believe Seedorf and Zambrotta's underpants!

I'M PUSHING DOWN AS HARD AS I CAN!

So that's how Inter's players squeeze out monster guffs!

MY BREATH HONKS!

Wales training is like Land Of The Giants for Robert Earnshaw!

I'LL TRY NOT TO HURT YOU!

AC Milan's Christian Abbiati needs to stop eating garlic bread at half-time!

MY MUM BRAIDED IT FOR ME!

This guy should be collecting the Worst Haircut Of The Year award, not a football!

LEGENDS

2011

RONALDO

FACTFILE!

Age: 26

Club: Real Madrid

Position: Winger

Value: £80 million

Country: Portugal

Footy Fact! Ronaldo was unstoppable in 2010-11! The trickster bagged 53 goals in 51 starts for Jose Mourinho's awesome side!

THE BIG QUIZ!

JOB SWAP!

Name the powerful Prem striker who's working as a traffic warden in this pic!

10 POINTS FOR CORRECT ANSWER

MY SCORE
10

BOGUS BADGES!

Which clubs do these badges belong to?

4 POINTS FOR EACH CORRECT ANSWER

MY SCORE
20

1. ....
2. ....

3. ....
4. ....
5. ....

5 QUESTIONS ON...

CRISTIANO RONALDO!

1 True or False? Real Madrid's trick machine was born in Spain but plays international footy for Portugal!

2 Which famous Portuguese club did Ronaldo play for between 2001 and 2003?

3 How many PFA Player Of The Year awards did the ex-Man. United superstar win – one, two or three?

4 How many La Liga goals did Ron smash home for Real Madrid last season – 25, 30, 35 or 40?

5 What famous shirt number does Ronaldo wear for Real Madrid – No.7, No.9 or No.10?

4 POINTS FOR EACH CORRECT ANSWER

MY SCORE
20

TROPHY DREAMER!

Which Chelsea midfielder is dreaming of winning the Champions League here?

THE DREAMING STAR IS...

10 POINTS FOR CORRECT ANSWER

MY SCORE
10

BRAINBUSTERS!

Answer these questions for a cool 20 points!

1 Who knocked Chelsea out of the 2010-11 Champions League?

2 Which Championship club plays its home games at St. Mary's?

3 Who scored more Prem goals last season – Dirk Kuyt or Didier Drogba?

4 Lethal Uruguay striker Edinson Cavani plays for which Serie A club?

5 How old is Real Madrid winger Angel di Maria – 21, 22 or 23 years old?

6 Which country did Uruguay beat in the 2011 Copa America final?

7 Which team did AFC Wimbledon beat to win promotion to League 2?

8 How much did Aston Villa sign Charles N'Zogbia for back in July?

9 Which La Liga club did David de Gea join Man. United from in June?

10 Which Premier League team finished tenth in 2010-11?

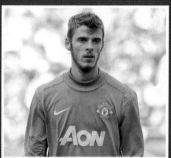

2 POINTS FOR EACH CORRECT ANSWER

MY SCORE 20

FLASHBACK!

5 POINTS FOR EACH CORRECT ANSWER

MY SCORE 20

Which European megastars will want to forget these dodgy old pictures?

THE EURO STAR IS...

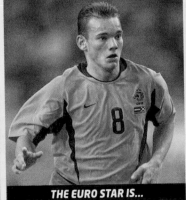

THE EURO STAR IS...

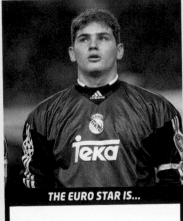

THE EURO STAR IS...

THE EURO STAR IS...

ANSWERS PAGE 94

they said wot?

MATCH checks out the craziest footy quotes we heard in 2011!

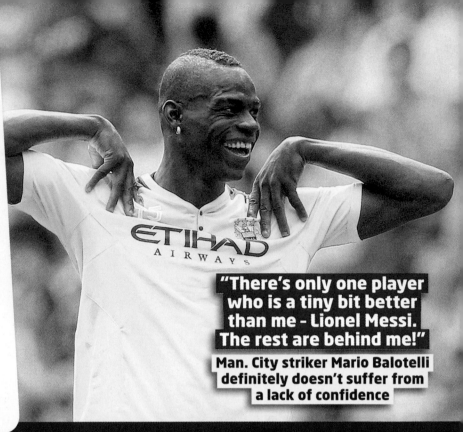

"There's only one player who is a tiny bit better than me - Lionel Messi. The rest are behind me!"

Man. City striker Mario Balotelli definitely doesn't suffer from a lack of confidence

"Leeds could have got a third and another one after that to make it three!"

With Leeds 2-1 up against Portsmouth, crazy Sky Sports pundit Chris Kamara suddenly forgets how to add up

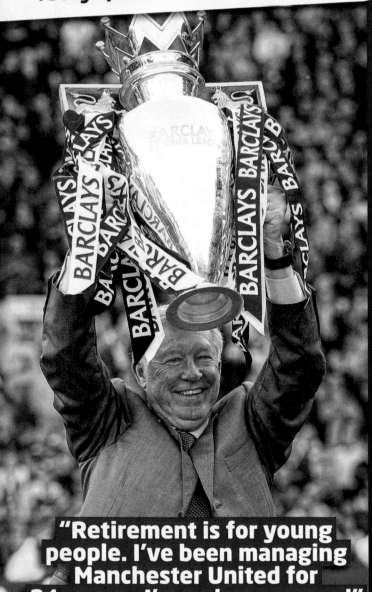

"Retirement is for young people. I've been managing Manchester United for 24 years - I'm a phenomenon!"

Sir Alex Ferguson months before winning a record 19th title

"At least Drogba is giving me some points for my fantasy team!"

Cesc Fabregas looks on the bright side after watching Chelsea thump Bolton 4-0 back in January

"Hate it when you're driving and the lorry in front has a sticker saying 'How is my driving?'... makes me want to call and say POOR!"

Arsenal midfielder Jack Wilshere rants about dodgy lorry drivers on Twitter

"Benni McCarthy was a big fat mistake. Rather than the super scorer we hoped for, we acquired a super-size player devoted to filling his belly more than filling the net!"

West Ham vice-chairman Karen Brady slams striker McCarthy

"If you had anyone to put money on to score a penalty it would be Ian Harte. He's absolutely sensational with his left foot. He steps up... and hits the post!"

Sky Sports' John Salako won't be banking on defender Ian Harte to score from the spot again

"A few people are calling it the first twansfer! I'll be retweeting the ones that came up with the name Kieran Agard. They'll be taking the credit!"

Yeovil boss Terry Skiverton thanks fans for their signing suggestions on Twitter after landing Agard

"There's nothing to do in Manchester! There's two restaurants and everything's small. It rains all the time, you can't go anywhere!"

Argentina striker Carlos Tevez seems to have had enough of his time at Man. City

MATCH GOES... TIME TR

1 YEAR AGO...

England's bid to host the 2018 World Cup ended in disaster as the tournament was given to Russia! Even **David Beckham** and Prince William couldn't persuade FIFA, as England only got two votes!

2 YEARS AGO...

After just 18 months in the job, Man. City sacked their manager Mark Hughes! The mega-rich club appointed former Inter Milan, Lazio and Fiorentina gaffer **Roberto Mancini** as his replacement!

3 YEARS AGO...

After failing to qualify for Euro 2008, England named **Fabio Capello** as their new manager! On taking the post, the former AC Milan and Real Madrid boss announced it would be his last job in football!

5 YEARS AGO...

Defender **Moritz Volz** scored a landmark goal in Fulham's 2-2 draw with rivals Chelsea! Volzy latched on to a long throw and smashed home the Premier League's 15,000th goal!

10 YEARS AGO...

A decade ago Man. United were having a terrible season! After six defeats in seven games, The Red Devils were ninth in the Prem! They went on to finish third, ten points behind champions **Arsenal**!

RAVELLING!

Here's the biggest festive footy stories from down the years!

14 YEARS AGO...

Liverpool signed USA keeper **Brad Friedel** from Columbus Crew for just £1 million! Friedel only made 31 appearances before moving to Blackburn on a free transfer in November 2000!

25 YEARS AGO...

Sir Alex Ferguson won his first ever away match as Man. United boss on Boxing Day! Forward Norman Whiteside scored the only goal of the game to sink massive rivals Liverpool!

20 YEARS AGO...

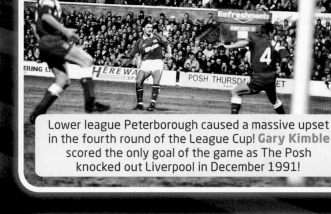

Lower league Peterborough caused a massive upset in the fourth round of the League Cup! **Gary Kimble** scored the only goal of the game as The Posh knocked out Liverpool in December 1991!

24 YEARS AGO...

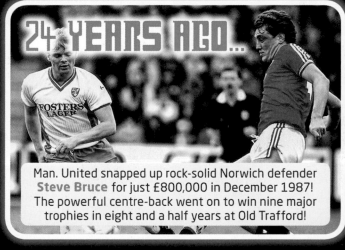

Man. United snapped up rock-solid Norwich defender **Steve Bruce** for just £800,000 in December 1987! The powerful centre-back went on to win nine major trophies in eight and a half years at Old Trafford!

100 YEARS AGO...

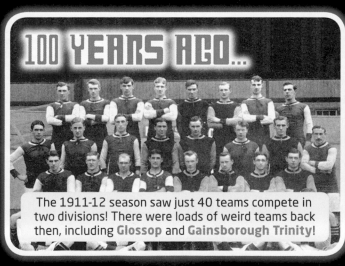

The 1911-12 season saw just 40 teams compete in two divisions! There were loads of weird teams back then, including **Glossop** and **Gainsborough Trinity**!

NEW STARS TO WATCH!

MATCH reveals the best young players on the planet who'll be ripping it up in 2012!

Juan Iturbe

He's the new...
Lionel Messi

Club: *Porto* **Age:** *18*

Position: *Forward*

Form guide: Look out for the star of Argentina's Under-20 World Cup squad! 'The Little Flea' joined Porto last summer and is shaping up to be a world-class playmaker, just like Barcelona legend Lionel Messi!

Style of play: With two quick feet, silky dribbling and a powerful left foot, Iturbe loves driving at defenders and ripping the net!

Career highlight: Iturbe ran from the halfway line, beat three Chile players and tucked the ball home in the Under-20 World Cup qualifiers!

STAT ATTACK

Speed		9
Dribbling		9
Shooting		8
Power		7

Erik Lamela

He's the new...
Ashley Young

Club: *Roma* **Age:** *19*

Position: *Winger*

Form guide: Roma beat off competition from Liverpool, Spurs and Barça to Lamela's signature last summer! He scored four goals in 2010-11 as River Plate were relegated for the first time ever!

Style of play: Lamela leaves defenders for dust with his lightning-quick runs down the left wing! Look out for the Argentina wonderkid in Serie A this season!

Career highlight: He made his Argentina debut in a 4-2 friendly win over Paraguay back in May!

STAT ATTACK

Speed		9
Tricks		8
Movement		8
Crossing		8

Philippe Coutinho

He's the new...
Wesley Sneijder

Club: *Inter Milan* **Age:** *19*

Position: *Midfielder*

Form Guide: Coutinho only made his debut for Inter Milan last year! He went on to make ten starts in 2010-11 and scored an awesome free-kick against Fiorentina!

Style of play: Coutinho is an expert at beating full-backs and playing through balls! The young Brazilian even opens up the play with awesome cross-field passes!

Career highlight: The quality playmaker scored a goal and set up two others as Brazil beat Austria 3-0 in the Under-20 World Cup!

STAT ATTACK
Passing	9
Vision	8
Crossing	8
Speed	8

James Rodriguez

He's the new...
Cristiano Ronaldo

Club: *Porto* **Age:** *20*

Position: *Winger*

Form guide: The Colombian made 24 appearances last season as Porto won the league, cup and Europa League! He's a free-kick expert, just like Cristiano Ronaldo!

Style of play: Rodriguez's pace and tricks cause nightmares for defenders, but he's also deadly in the box! The Colombia star is ice-cool at finishing one-on-ones!

Career highlight: Rodriguez hit an incredible hat-trick as Porto thrashed Vitoria Guimaraes 6-2 in the 2011 Portuguese Cup final!

STAT ATTACK
Finishing	9
Crossing	8
Passing	8
Strength	7

Josh McEachran

He's the new...
Jack Wilshere

Club: *Chelsea* **Age:** *18*

Position: *Midfielder*

Form guide: McEachran could be a future superstar after making his first-team debut last season! The England Under-21 star was named Chelsea's Young Player Of The Year!

Style of play: Look out for him this season! The movement and passing of this Chelsea wonderkid makes him a world-class talent!

Career highlight: Josh was in the team that won the Under-17 European Championship in 2010! He scored in England's first group game against the Czech Republic!

STAT ATTACK
Passing	9
Vision	9
Heading	7
Shooting	7

John Flanagan

He's the new...
Glen Johnson

Club: *Liverpool* **Age:** *18*

Position: *Right-back*

Form guide: Flanagan broke into Liverpool's first team last season after making his name in The Reds' academy – the same place where legend Jamie Carragher started out!

Style of play: Wingers hate battling with Flanagan! He's a rock-hard right-back who's strong on the ball, awesome in the air and makes tons of crunching tackles!

Career highlight: Flanagan played the full 90 minutes of his first-team debut when Liverpool beat Man. City 3-0 last April!

STAT ATTACK
Tackling		9
Heading		8
Power		8
Speed		7

Julio Gomez

He's the new...
Nani

Club: *Pachuca* **Age:** *17*

Position: *Winger*

Form guide: What a year Gomez has had! The Mexico winger only made his league debut in January, but went on to win the Golden Ball at the Under-17 World Cup!

Style of play: Gomez uses tons of tricks and rapid bursts of speed to turn defenders inside out! We'd love to see him come to the Prem!

Career highlight: Scoring three goals as Mexico won the Under-17 World Cup in front of their home fans! Gomez and his team-mates beat Uruguay 2-0 in the final!

STAT ATTACK
Tricks		9
Shooting		8
Passing		8
Speed		8

Carl Jenkinson

He's the new...
Bacary Sagna

Club: *Arsenal* **Age:** *19*

Position: *Right-back*

Form guide: Arsenal snapped up the ex-Charlton defender in June for £1 million! His ambition is to replace Bacary Sagna at right-back!

Style of play: Jenkinson can play at right-back or in the centre of defence! He's strong, likes to go forward and captained Finland's Under-19 team last season!

Career highlight: Jenkinson won't forget the crazy own goal he scored against Cologne in pre-season! He lobbed Wojciech Szczesny from outside the area!

STAT ATTACK
Movement		9
Tackling		8
Strength		7
Passing		7

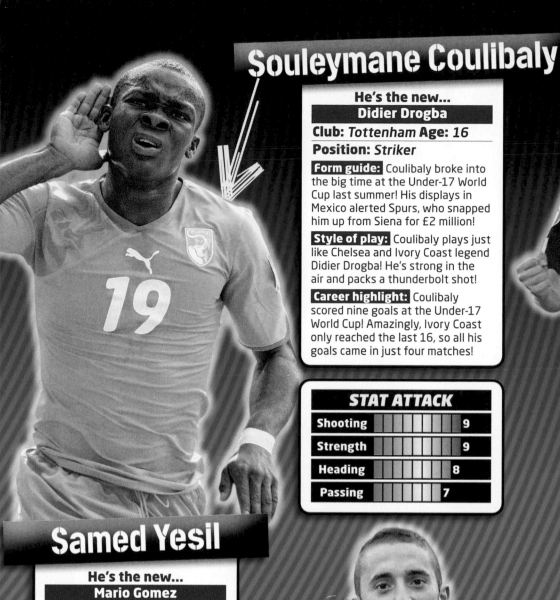

Souleymane Coulibaly

He's the new...
Didier Drogba

Club: *Tottenham* **Age:** *16*
Position: *Striker*

Form guide: Coulibaly broke into the big time at the Under-17 World Cup last summer! His displays in Mexico alerted Spurs, who snapped him up from Siena for £2 million!

Style of play: Coulibaly plays just like Chelsea and Ivory Coast legend Didier Drogba! He's strong in the air and packs a thunderbolt shot!

Career highlight: Coulibaly scored nine goals at the Under-17 World Cup! Amazingly, Ivory Coast only reached the last 16, so all his goals came in just four matches!

STAT ATTACK
Shooting	9
Strength	9
Heading	8
Passing	7

Samed Yesil

He's the new...
Mario Gomez

Club: *Bayer Leverkusen*
Age: *17* **Position:** *Striker*

Form guide: Watch out for Yesil in the Bundesliga this season! The Germany striker was joint-top scorer at the Under-17 European Championship last summer!

Style of play: Germany's young striker is an expert at racing on to pinpoint passes and blasting the ball into the back of the net! He's been linked with a move to Arsenal!

Career highlight: Yesil opened the scoring in the Under-17 European Championship final against Holland back in May!

STAT ATTACK
Shooting	9
Speed	9
Heading	7
Strength	7

Christian Eriksen

He's the new...
Rafael van der Vaart

Club: *Ajax* **Age:** *19*
Position: *Midfielder*

Form guide: Eriksen won't ever forget 2010-11! Ajax's playmaker scored eight goals in 29 starts, won the Eredivisie title and was named Young Player Of The Year!

Style of play: Eriksen is going to be one of the stars of European footy for years! The Denmark international has an amazing box-to-box engine and his defence-splitting passes are world-class!

Career highlight: Eriksen was the youngest player at the 2010 World Cup in South Africa!

STAT ATTACK
Passing	9
Vision	9
Shooting	8
Speed	8

THE BIG QUIZ!

HEAD OF TWO HALVES!

Which Prem bosses have had their heads mashed together?

5 POINTS FOR EACH CORRECT ANSWER

MY SCORE **10**

TOP HALF...

BOTTOM HALF...

GOAL MACHINES!

Name these Champions League goal kings from last season!

1	Barcelona 12 goals	
2	Bayern Munich 8 goals	
3	Inter Milan 8 goals	
4	Schalke 5 goals	
5	AC Milan 4 goals	

2 POINTS FOR EACH CORRECT ANSWER

MY SCORE **10**

5 QUESTIONS ON... GARETH BALE!

1 True or False? The speedy winger plays international footy for Republic Of Ireland!

2 Which top Championship club did Tottenham sign Bale from back in 2007?

3 How many goals did Bale score for Spurs in the Champions League last season?

4 What footy award did he win last season – Prem Golden Boot or PFA Player Of The Year?

5 Which team did Gareth score a hat-trick against in the 2010-11 Champions League?

2 POINTS FOR EACH CORRECT ANSWER

MY SCORE **10**

NATIONAL TEAM HEROES!

Name the countries these Prem stars play for!

2 POINTS FOR EACH CORRECT ANSWER

MY SCORE **10**

Barry Bannan

Marouane Fellaini

Cheik Tiote

Danny Collins

Asamoah Gyan

WORDFIT!

CLEVERLEY

2 POINTS FOR EACH CORRECT ANSWER

MY SCORE 40

Anderson	Evra	Giggs	Owen	Smalling
Berbatov	Fabio	Hernandez	Park	Valencia
Carrick	Ferdinand	Jones	Rafael	Vidic
De Gea	Fletcher	Nani	Rooney	Young

4 POINTS FOR EACH CORRECT ANSWER

MY SCORE 20

CLUB CAPTAINS!

Can you name the skippers at these massive European teams?

THE ROONEY STORY

MATCH LOOKS BACK AT THE BIG STORIES FROM THE MAN. UNITED AND ENGLAND STRIKER'S CAREER SO FAR!

WAYNE MARK ROONEY WAS BORN ON OCTOBER 24, 1985, IN CROXTETH, LIVERPOOL. HE GREW UP SUPPORTING EVERTON AND JOINED THE CLUB WHEN HE WAS NINE. ROONEY WAS A GOALSCORING SENSATION FROM A YOUNG AGE AND SCORED EIGHT GOALS IN THEIR RUN TO THE 2002 FA YOUTH CUP FINAL!

ROONEY MADE HIS PREM DEBUT AGAINST SPURS IN AUGUST 2002! WAYNE HIT THE HEADLINES TWO MONTHS LATER WHEN HE SCORED HIS FIRST PREMIER LEAGUE GOAL – AN UNSTOPPABLE 25-YARD STRIKE AGAINST ARSENAL FIVE DAYS BEFORE HIS 17TH BIRTHDAY!

I HOPE WAYNE DOESN'T LET RIP AGAIN!

AFTER SCORING NINE PREM GOALS IN 2003-04, MAN. UNITED BEAT NEWCASTLE TO SIGN ROONEY FOR £25.6 MILLION! WAYNE MARKED HIS DEBUT IN SENSATIONAL STYLE AS HE SCORED A HAT-TRICK AGAINST FENERBAHÇE IN THE CHAMPIONS LEAGUE!

THERE'S TWO MORE TO COME!

ROONEY HAD AN UNFORGETTABLE 2002-03! HE WAS CROWNED THE BBC YOUNG SPORTS PERSONALITY OF THE YEAR, BECAME THE YOUNGEST EVER SENIOR ENGLAND INTERNATIONAL IN A FRIENDLY AGAINST AUSTRALIA AND FINISHED THE SEASON WITH SIX GOALS IN 14 PREM STARTS!

"I NEVER TOUCHED HIM!"

"SEE YA, WAZZA!"

MORE RECORDS FELL AT EURO 2004 WHEN ROONEY BECAME THE TOURNAMENT'S YOUNGEST GOALSCORER AFTER NETTING TWICE AGAINST SWITZERLAND! THE FOLLOWING SEASON HE WON THE PFA PLAYER OF THE YEAR AWARD AND WAS THE RED DEVILS' TOP SCORER WITH 11 PREM GOALS!

ROONEY WON HIS FIRST TROPHY IN FEBRUARY 2006, SCORING TWICE AGAINST WIGAN IN THE CARLING CUP FINAL! HE BATTLED BACK FROM A BROKEN METATARSAL TO PLAY AT THE WORLD CUP IN GERMANY, BUT COULDN'T FIND THE NET AND WAS SENT OFF AGAINST PORTUGAL IN THE QUARTER-FINALS!

"HAVE SOME OF THAT, ROMAN!"

MORE SILVERWARE FOLLOWED IN 2006-07 AS ROONEY SCORED 14 GOALS TO HELP UNITED WIN THE TITLE BY SIX POINTS! WAYNE HAD AN INJURY-HIT START TO THE 2008 SEASON, BUT BATTLED BACK TO WIN THE PREM AND THE CHAMPIONS LEAGUE AGAINST CHELSEA!

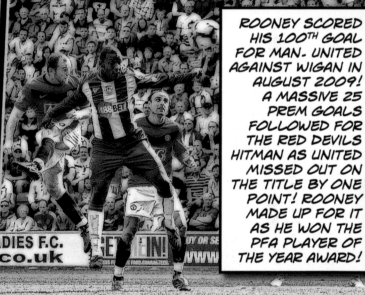

ROONEY SCORED HIS 100TH GOAL FOR MAN. UNITED AGAINST WIGAN IN AUGUST 2009! A MASSIVE 25 PREM GOALS FOLLOWED FOR THE RED DEVILS HITMAN AS UNITED MISSED OUT ON THE TITLE BY ONE POINT! ROONEY MADE UP FOR IT AS HE WON THE PFA PLAYER OF THE YEAR AWARD!

"I KNOW WE WERE RUBBISH!"

BIG THINGS WERE EXPECTED FROM ROONEY AT THE 2010 WORLD CUP IN SOUTH AFRICA, BUT THINGS DIDN'T GO TO PLAN! WAYNE FAILED TO FIND THE NET IN ALL FOUR GAMES AS ENGLAND WERE THRASHED BY GERMANY AND CRASHED OUT IN THE LAST 16!

ROONEY HAD AN ASTONISHING 2010-11 SEASON! EVERYONE THOUGHT HE WAS GOING TO QUIT THE CLUB BEFORE SIGNING A NEW FIVE-YEAR DEAL, WINNING A FOURTH PREMIER LEAGUE TITLE AND REACHING THE CHAMPIONS LEAGUE FINAL! HIS VOLLEY AGAINST MAN. CITY BACK IN FEBRUARY WAS ONE OF THE BEST GOALS EVER!

= CLASSIC MATCH 2011 =

 **Barcelona**
Pedro 27; Messi 54; Villa 69

3 : 1

Man. United
Rooney 34

Date: May 28 **Stadium:** Wembley **Tournament:** Champions League final

What happened? Barça lifted the European Cup for the fourth time after a pulsating Champions League final at Wembley! Pedro slotted the Spanish side ahead, before Wayne Rooney equalised with a stunning finish for The Red Devils! After the break, Barça were untouchable, with goals by Lionel Messi and David Villa sealing the win!

QUESTION 1

True or False? Pep Guardiola played in the Barcelona side that won the European Cup at Wembley in 1992!

....

QUESTION 2

How many goals did striker Wayne Rooney score in the Champions League last season - four, five or six?

....

QUESTION 3

In what year did Man. United last win the Champions League trophy?

....

QUESTION 4

Which Man. United legend retired after last season's Champions League final against Barcelona?

....

QUESTION 5

Name the former Man. United defender who played for Barcelona in this final!

....

QUESTION 6

Which Barcelona megastar wore the No.6 shirt in last season's final?

....

HERE COMES 2012!

MATCH looks into our crystal football to preview the year ahead!

Allianz ⑪ Arena

Champions League!

Can an English team stop Barça winning a fifth Champo League final, or will Pep Guardiola's side conquer Europe again? The final takes place at Munich's Allianz Arena on Saturday, May 19!

Transfer Window!

We can't wait for Prem clubs to start splashing the cash in January! If it beats the record-breaking deals we saw in 2011, it's going to be an awesome few weeks of mega moves and world-class gossip!

Africa Cup Of Nations!

The first major tournament of the year kicks off on January 21 in Gabon and Equatorial Guinea! Look out for Premier League stars Didier Drogba, Gervinho, Yaya Toure and Asamoah Gyan!

Euro 2012!

If you've not read our preview of the tournament on page 50, then head over there right now! Can England forget the disappointment of the 2010 World Cup and finally bring home some silverware, or will it be the same old sorry story?

El Clasico!

No teams will be able to touch Barça and Real Madrid in La Liga this season! There's a crunch title-decider on April 22 – whoever wins that match has a big chance of bagging the Spanish title!

Europa League!

Bucharest's quality national stadium in Romania will host the 2011 Europa League final on Wednesday, May 9! Can an English side lift the trophy for the first time since Liverpool in 2001?

Title Fight!

There are some amazing Premier League matches heading your way in April, as the race for the title hots up! Arsenal battle Chelsea, and Man. City take on arch rivals Man. United with just a few games of the season left!

London 2012!

Team GB's men's and women's teams will be battling it out for gold at the Olympics next summer! The action kicks off at the end of July, with the finals taking place at Wembley!

World Cup Qualifiers!

The road to Brazil 2014 begins next autumn and MATCH will be following all the action! Look out for Scotland and Wales going head-to-head in Group A, and England's massive clashes against Montenegro, Ukraine and Poland in Group H!

100% FOOTY ACTION EVERY WEEK!

ROCK-HARD QUIZZES!

FOOTY GOSSIP!

FUNNY PICS!

ALL-STAR FANTASY FOOTY!

GREAT COMPETITIONS!

HEADS-UP CHALLENGE!

CARROLL PLAYER POSTERS!

QUIZ ANSWERS!

★ THE BIG QUIZ ★
PAGES 10-11

SPORT SWITCH!
Peter Crouch.

BOGUS BADGES!
1. Norwich; 2. Real Madrid;
3. AC Milan; 4. Rangers;
5. Liverpool.

DAVID LUIZ QUIZ!
1. Benfica; 2. Brazil;
3. £21 million; 4. Two;
5. Man. United.

WHO AM I?
Yaya Toure.

NAME THE TEAM!

1. T. Walcott; 2. J. Milner;
3. J. Terry; 4. R. Ferdinand;
5. D. Bent; 6. F. Lampard;
7. S. Parker; 8. A. Cole;
9. J. Hart; 10. G. Johnson;
11. J. Wilshere.

FLASHBACK!
Andy Carroll; Peter
Odemwingie; Michael
Dawson & Michael Carrick.

★ WORDSEARCH ★
PAGE 12

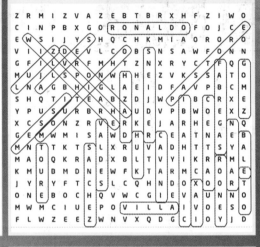

★ EXTRA-TIME ★
PAGE 20

1. Wales; 2. True;
3. Man. City & Man. United;
4. 29; 5. Vauxhall;
6. £56 million; 7. The Albert;
8. Gus Poyet; 9. Ivory Coast;
10. Man. United; 11. Fifth;
12. Mark Hughes;
13. Umbro; 14. Three
- Aston Villa, Sunderland &
Tottenham; 15. True;
16. Sergio Batista; 17. Nani;
18. Notts County; 19. Frank
Lampard & Darren Bent;
20. 19; 21. Braga; 22. No.6;
23. Fernando Torres;
24. Blackpool; 25. Crewe.

★ THE BIG QUIZ ★
PAGES 40-41

FLIPPED!
Dirk Kuyt.

MAN. UNITED QUIZ!
1. True; 2. 19; 3. Nike; 4. Rio
Ferdinand; 5. £16 million.

DARREN BENT QUIZ!
1. Ipswich; 2. Charlton;
3. Uruguay; 4. Switzerland;
5. £24 million.

STAR JUMBLE!
Phil Neville; Peter
Odemwingie; Wesley
Sneijder; Jack Wilshere
& Karim Benzema.

WORDFIT!

EURO GIANTS!
Lorient - France;
Stuttgart - Germany;
Fiorentina - Italy;
Ajax - Holland;
Real Mallorca - Spain.

★ WORDFIT ★
PAGE 44

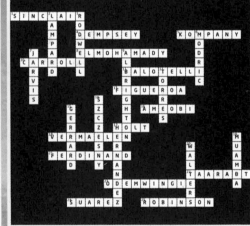

★ EXTRA-TIME ★
PAGE 48

1. False - they play at The
Hawthorns; 2. Newcastle;
3. Mexico; 4. Italy;
5. Thomas; 6. Leicester;
7. Hartlepool; 8. Malouda;
9. True; 10. LA Galaxy;
11. Shay Given; 12. Wayne
Rooney; 13. Kenny Miller;
14. 34; 15. Nine; 16. True;
17. Birmingham; 18. Reebok
Stadium; 19. Watford &
Reading; 20. The Canaries;
21. Gareth Bale; 22. Xavi;
23. Stewart Downing;
24. Stoke; 25. False - he's
won it with two clubs.

★ THE BIG QUIZ ★
PAGES 56-57

SPORT SWITCH!
Leighton Baines.

FELLAINI'S BARBERSHOP!
Andres Iniesta.

WALCOTT QUIZ!
1. 2006; 2. Aston Villa;
3. Chelsea; 4. Croatia;
5. No.14.

STADIUM GAME!
1. Rangers; 2. Real Madrid;
3. Newcastle; 4. QPR;
5. Wigan.

CROSSWORD!

TRANSFER TRACKER!
2004-08: Newcastle;
2008-10: Aston Villa.

★ THE BIG QUIZ ★
PAGES 74-75

JOB SWAP!
Kevin Davies.

BOGUS BADGES!
1. Cardiff;
2. Everton;
3. Sheffield United;
4. Newcastle;
5. Hearts.

CRISTIANO RONALDO QUIZ!
1. False; 2. Sporting Lisbon;
3. Two; 4. 40; 5. No.7.

TROPHY DREAMER!
Ramires.

BRAINBUSTERS!
1. Man. United;
2. Southampton;
3. Dirk Kuyt; 4. Napoli;
5. 23; 6. Paraguay; 7. Luton;
8. £9.5 million; 9. Atletico
Madrid; 10. Sunderland.

FLASHBACK!
Raul; Wesley Sneijder;
Iker Casillas & Mesut Ozil.

★ THE BIG QUIZ ★
PAGES 84-85

HEAD OF TWO HALVES!
Neil Warnock & Roy Hodgson.

GOAL MACHINES!
1. Messi; 2. Gomez; 3. Eto'o;
4. Raul; 5. Ibrahimovic.

GARETH BALE QUIZ!
1. False; 2. Southampton;
3. Four; 4. PFA Player Of
The Year; 5. Inter Milan.

NATIONAL HEROES!
Bannan - Scotland;
Fellaini - Belgium;
Tiote - Ivory Coast;
Collins - Wales;
Gyan - Ghana.

WORDFIT!

CLUB CAPTAINS!
Real Madrid - Iker Casillas;
AC Milan - M. Ambrosini;
Juventus - Alessandro Del
Piero; Barcelona - Carles
Puyol; Chelsea - John Terry.

MY TOTAL: /800